Oracle of the Obvious:

secrets of

common sense

leadership

By

Dena Hurst

Raymond D. Jorgensen

Copyright © 2009 by Jorgensen Learning Center

Published by JLC Publishing

Illustrations by Brenda Green
Edited and designed by Kathryn Marion
Printed by Voice of Prosperity, LLC

Printed in the United States of America

ISBN 978-0-615-32840-9

Acknowledgments

We wish to thank those who are taking the time to learn more about leading living systems. We're sure you realize that leading anyone, including self, is challenging. It takes discipline, focus, and commitment to the work. The goal of any leadership endeavor is to enhance our capacity to support people in accomplishing their dreams.

Since this book emanated from the collective feedback from many, many clients and individuals, it would be impossible to list all of those caring and concerned leaders. Be assured that we appreciate every word and suggestion and every opportunity to share our work and practice with you.

Many thanks for taking the time to peruse *Oracle of the Obvious: secrets of common sense leadership*. One of the values of our organization is continuous improvement. All of the authors would enjoy your comments and feedback so that we can improve this product to better serve you. Feel free to contact us at your leisure or at any time in need at the Jorgensen Learning Center.

~ Yours in Service in Learning

Jorgensen Learning Center
Success is in the conversation.

2108 Park Avenue ⬦ PMB #105 ⬦ Orange Park, FL 32073

Phone: 904.264.9200 ⬦ Fax: 904.297.3764 ⬦

www.GOJLC.com

Part 1

Learning Conversations
page 7

Foreword

Despite the current popularity of "systems thinking" and "organizational learning" in both the private and public sectors, there are painfully few books on the subject that offer examples of how to actually engage in systems work in a practical way. Jorgensen and Hurst offer just such a book, one that puts into everyday language the disciplines necessary for engaging in conversations that matter, conversations that can be carried out daily in an effort to bring forth the voice of everyone living and working in a system. As the book so aptly demonstrates, these conversations and voices offer the most significant opportunity for growth and, ultimately, success as defined by participants in any system.

The book begins with one of the most critical elements necessary for real learning conversations: the discipline of listening. Many of us can relate to the space shuttle Challenger story shared in the Introduction, and the questions that went through our minds, such as, "How could this happen?" In my case, the disbelief was voiced as, "This can't be happening." As Ray went on to describe the story behind the story, I recalled one of the most powerful experiences in my professional career, an experience where I thought I was so connected to the system I was leading that the people in the system would tell me anything. What I found out after I left the system was that there were things happening that were never shared with me—things that, if I had known them, would have caused me to act and lead in a significantly different way.

The book continues with the components of meaningful learning conversations and the disciplines necessary to lead these conversations in an effective way. Without these disciplines—including speaking from the heart, suspension of certainty, holding space for differences, and more—real learning conversations will not occur.

For me, the piece on voice is most critical. I believe we have all been in "meetings" when the appointed leader was sharing the goals and plans for implementation of a new initiative, and we said to ourselves, "That's never going to work because. . ." Yet the environment was not secure enough for us to share our thoughts openly. We felt as if either the leader did not want to know what we thought or (perhaps more damaging to the system) we felt that if we held a view contrary to the leader and shared it publicly, we risked ridicule, marginalization, or worse.

It has been my experience that unfiltered voice—the act of hearing directly from people—may be the most powerful tool available to leaders in all systems. What do people really think, what are we missing, and what are the unintended consequences of our actions? How will those working in the system carry an initiative forward if they do not believe in its viability or have not been a part of its development?

Jorgensen's main point regarding voice is that facilitating voice for all engages all. When people are engaged, they bring their minds and hearts to the work of the system. They become part of the total organization. They become committed to the organization's work because they were a part of determining the organization's work. Jorgensen explains this in a way that everyone can understand. He shares his insights, personal experiences, and thoughts about real-life implementation, allowing the reader the confidence to engage in this work daily.

When I first began this journey nearly two decades ago, the primary challenge for me was keeping the conversation alive on a daily basis. Ray Jorgensen and Dena Hurst have written a book that supports keeping real, tangible learning conversations alive whether one is just starting their conversational leadership journey or is decades into the process.

The nature of disciplines is that if they are not practiced and reflected upon, they are lost. In recognition of this, they have developed a structure in support of one's personal journey. The journal provided prompts that support the reader's reflection as they engage in this work on a regular basis, prompts that will benefit both novices and the most experienced alike, as without personal reflection there can be no personal growth.

Donald A. James, Ed.D.
Chief Executive Officer and Superintendent of Schools
Center Moriches School District

Author's Note

Duke Huan was reading in the upper part of his hall and Wheelwright Flat was hewing a wheel in the lower part. Setting aside his hammer and chisel, the wheelwright went to the upper part of the hall and inquired of Duke Huan, saying, "I venture to ask what words Your Highness is reading?"

"The words of the sages," said the duke.

"Are the sages still alive?"

"They're already dead," said the duke.

"Then what my lord is reading are merely the dregs of the ancients."

"How can you, a wheelwright, comment upon what I am reading?" asked Duke Huan. "If you can explain yourself, all right. If you cannot explain yourself, you shall die."

"I look at it from my own occupation," said Wheelwright Flat. "If the spokes are loose, they'll fit sweet as a whistle but the wheel won't be solid. If they're too tight, you won't be able to insert them no matter how hard you try. To make them neither too loose nor too tight is something you sense in your hand and feel in your heart. There's a knack to it that can't be put into words. I haven't been able to teach it to my own son, and my son hasn't been able to learn it from me.

That's why I'm still hewing wheels after seventy years. When they died, the ancients took with them what they could not transmit. So what you are reading are the dregs of the ancients."

-- Zhuangzi

There is a knack in every discipline that moves it from the perfunctory parroting of a method or practice to an elegant use of protocol or method; an elegant use that moves people from simple response to meaning. It is our most sincere hope that these words, although not "knackful" in themselves, provide an ignition of the souls of men and women looking to enhance the impact of their leadership practice.

Because leadership intends to educe or draw greatness out of those we lead, each chapter asks the reader to look inward and draw upon those sleeping resources. Peter Senge states that there are three leadership capabilities simultaneously in play: aspiration, effective conversations, and seeing the whole. We invite you to look for these three disciplines throughout the book.

An introduction to

1. Why Conversation Matters

Even one person can have a sense of dialogue within himself, if the spirit of the dialogue is present. The picture or image that this derivation suggests is of a stream of meaning flowing among and through us and between us. (David Bohm)

The day is forever imprinted in my memory, a day that will live with me with unrivaled clarity. I was principal of Charlotte High School, sitting at my desk in my office, having just made morning rounds to be sure the students made it to classes on time. Books and papers were piled on the desk and the credenza behind me. The bustling of the external office was a constant hum in the background. It was a morning like any other, with the exception of the event about to take place.

I was watching the small TV in the corner. It showed me a beautiful south Florida day: clear blue skies bathed in pure sunlight. NASA engineers and technicians were quietly working through a checklist, preparing the space shuttle Challenger for yet another launch. The scene on the television was controlled—a quiet voice much like that of a golf announcer readying the audience for the countdown. I could see the shuttle braced to the rocket that would launch it into space and the scaffolding that supported the shuttle in its upright position. I could hear the powerful rumble of the rocket, see the smoke and flames pouring from beneath it. The launch of a shuttle is not a novel event in central and south Florida, but it is an awesome one nonetheless.

The countdown began with a calming voice reciting numbers from 10 to 1. Then liftoff. I could feel the collective sigh of relief of every Floridian connected to this magnificent show through the miracle of television and could see the tension drop from the NASA launch crew.

And then, no sooner it seemed than the shuttle had left the ground and begun to fly on its own power, a mighty explosion rocked the sky. I stared in disbelief at the screen, searching vainly for the movement of the shuttle, expecting to see it emerge from the clouds of smoke. Utter confusion for seconds, minutes, as reporters, engineers, by-standers, and television viewers tried to make sense of what they had just witnessed. There was a refusal to believe what was surely impossible, as if such a tragedy could not occur under the protective gaze of all of us who were watching. Reluctant acceptance settled in as the smoke cleared and the shuttle remained nowhere in sight. Confirmation by NASA that yes, indeed, the space shuttle Challenger had exploded. In the blink of an eye, 73 seconds after liftoff, before thousands of people who could do nothing but watch helplessly, the shuttle and crew were gone.

No one who watched the explosion firsthand will ever forget it. For those whose family or friends were on board, there is probably no sadder moment. I had met Christa McAuliffe, teacher of the year from New Hampshire, at a conference and considered her a friend. But beyond the grief I felt for my friend and for the other astronauts, this was a life-altering moment. In the coming months, as the investigations began and the cause of the shuttle explosion was revealed, my life's work was defined.

It was publicly disclosed that the cause of the explosion was a defect in an O-ring seal of the solid-fuel rocket. Most reports state that the O-ring failed because of a design flaw coupled with unusually cold weather. However, also reported at the time, but not as easily recalled, are the other contributing factors. Liftoff was postponed three times from January 22 to January 24…postponed an additional day due to bad weather at a secondary landing site…postponed one more day when the launch process was not completed in time to meet the liftoff window…and postponed one more day when a hatch closing fixture could not be removed from the hatch. While repairs were made, high winds caused yet another two-hour delay. Finally, five days after its originally scheduled launch, Challenger went up.

When asked by auditors whether Challenger should have been launched, virtually every engineer interviewed who worked on the project answered, "No." Individually, they each stated that the launch should never have taken place. But when they were asked by supervisors during the project, they could not truthfully communicate up the chain of command. A reason for this was given by Richard Feynman, a physicist and member of the panel that researched the Challenger disaster, in his *Personal Observations on the Reliability of the Shuttle.*

> *Finally, if we are to replace standard numerical probability usage with engineering judgment, why do we find such an enormous disparity between the management estimate and the judgment of the engineers? It would appear that, for whatever purpose, be it for internal or external consumption, the management of NASA exaggerates the reliability of its product, to the point of fantasy.*

Although working as hard as they could to make the launch a success, the environment impeded those shuttle engineers from voicing their fears or concerns, much less question decisions made by those in authority. As is so often the case, when it is difficult to communicate vertically in the system, people become silent and do the best they can.

As a leader, I was astounded at this revelation. I have been in professional settings where speaking out was at the very least not encouraged—sometimes openly discouraged—so my shock was not that those engineers worked in such conditions. Rather, for the first time it struck me (in a most physical sense as well as the figurative sense) that when we allow voices to be silenced, lives are at stake. I wondered instantly when I had done the same thing and thought of all the professions that impact our safety and security…doctors and nurses, police officers and fire fighters, airplane pilots and bus drivers…and the list goes on.

Now expand this list to those professionals who impact our well-being…teachers and coaches, the utility company employees who keep our lights on and our water running, the park rangers who tend our public spaces, the elected officials who manage the business of our communities…and you see that *conversation matters*. Not talking at each other, sending memos, stumping. Deep and authentic conversation.

As leaders, I believe this is our real work, to convene and nurture conversations that matter. Due to client demand, this has become the focus of my work and of the Jorgensen Learning Center. My professional practice has always been, and is, more than just consulting. We are creating a model of leadership that can be applied across economic sectors and geographic borders. It is cross-generational and multi-cultural, and can touch everyone no matter the path they are on. It can do this because it reaches into that part of ourselves that is human—that part we share one with another.

The image we hold of the work of leaders is one of a journey. All of us as leaders—in our offices, our homes, our communities—are on a leadership journey, and it is a journey without end, through all seasons, through all time and space.

Our role in your journey, and in writing this book, is to serve as a guide, to show you markers along the way, offer a gentle push when you get stuck, and help you visualize possibilities as they unfold along your path.

PART ONE:
LEARNING CONVERSATIONS

Our research into the power of conversations began with reading David Bohm and Peter Senge. Ray and others were charged with learning about dialogue and the work being done at the Massachusetts Institute of Technology, specifically the Dialogos project. We were also fortunate to attend seminars led by Sue Miller Hurst, Paula Underwood, and Bill Isaacs, among others, all powerful dialogue facilitators.

Before attending those seminars, Ray and others gathered a group of colleagues and friends in a circle for a day to discuss Senge's writings on dialogue in The Fifth Discipline. He remembers this experience vividly. Everyone stared at him as he stumbled through an explanation of what dialogue meant. He had put in a couple hours of real effort when one gentleman said to the group, "What

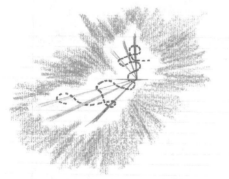

you're trying to explain sounds like what I remember growing up on a farm. At the end of the day, family and workers would sit on the front porch and talk about what they did that day and what needed to be done tomorrow, and they'd usually have some funny stories to share."

In sharing this experience we were struck by the sense of what a rich experience that must have been, to be among people caring for one another around their work. Yet we still weren't able to fully understand what that was or could be, much less how to create it—it took years more of disciplined practice and study before we were able to fully form the picture. We remain grateful for the work of Sue, Paula, and Bill. It is in honor of their work that we present this section on the five Learning Conversation Guidelines and show respect for the practice that has further taught us how to hold space for conversation.

A Learning Conversation is a conversation with the outcome of generating learning for those who participate. Not every conversation is, or need be, a Learning Conversation. But when we are in our leadership role (as CEO, teacher, parent, physician, political leader), our leadership conversations can be Learning Conversations.

Learning Conversations do not look or feel like other conversations. Learning Conversations go through phases where the energy and focus ebb and flow. The participants feel inspired, surprised, touched, uncomfortable, bored, quiet, satisfied, angry, confused, and more at different times during the conversations. Learning Conversations are the realm in which we as leaders do our work as a

Jorgensen Learning Center

shared field for developing common understanding and shared meaning.

Learning Conversations are governed by a set of Guidelines:

Listen deeply for understanding

Speak from the heart

Suspend certainty

Listen Speak Suspend Hold Slow !

Hold space for difference

Slow down the conversation

Though presented in a linear format, there is no linear order to these Guidelines. Each one grows from, and reinforces, the others.

Each Learning Conversation Guideline takes sustained, consistent practice if you are to release yourself from the habitual ways of thinking, speaking, and listening.

1.   Listen deeply for understanding

There are voices which we hear in solitude, but they grow faint and inaudible as we enter into the world. (Ralph Waldo Emerson)

When was the last time you were deeply heard?
Really…think about it.

A time when you know that what you were saying was the sole focus of the person listening.

What did it feel like? Put yourself in that moment and remain still. Now think about some of the adjectives that arose…and think about why you had those feelings.

To listen deeply for understanding is to listen from a place of peace
> of focus
>> of caring
>>> of learning.

It is listening to truly understand not just what the other person says, but more what they mean.

It is listening to the words, paying attention to the words chosen, to the words avoided, to the words repeated.

It is also listening to what is *not* said,
> and to the silence between the words.

It is listening because what the other person says *matters*.

It is listening because you believe that every voice should be heard.

It is listening without distraction, from others or yourself.

It is listening purely, with no thought being given to what should be said in response
> (because you trust that you will know what should be said when it is time to speak).

It is listening without judgment or blame.

It is listening without knowing the answers,
> or having to know the answers
> > or how to fix a problem.

Deep listening, listening for understanding, takes practice. More than active listening, listening for understanding comes from a place deep within us that bridges our separation from one another. Listening for understanding connects us, human being to human being, with all of the trappings of our daily lives—status, position, title, race, gender, religion—briefly suspended.

2. Speak from the heart

Go to your bosom:
Knock there and ask your heart what it doth
know. (William Shakespeare)

To speak from the heart is to give voice to the thoughts
inside you: questions, concerns, reflections, wonderings,
observations.

It is speaking for yourself, and yourself only...
 from your own experience,
  and from the moment.

It is speaking in order to further a conversation...
 not just to hear your own voice or to fill a silence.

It is speaking honestly.

It is avoiding defensiveness, blame or judgment.

It is acknowledging how you feel as you speak and listen,
 and sharing your feelings respectfully.

It is speaking to expand shared meaning.

Speaking from the heart lends transparency to the system.
It allows you to say what is on your heart in a way that
deepens your own learning and the learning of others.

Practicing this guideline, you will notice yourself becoming more adept at expressing what is important to you, and consequently feeling less often the tension of holding your tongue. You will find people responding in kind to you, sharing more honestly what they are thinking.

3.   Suspend certainty

*Loyalty to a petrified opinion never yet broke a
chain or freed a human soul. (Mark Twain)*

Imagine exhaling all of your attitudes,
biases, beliefs, and assumptions
(hereafter referred to as ABBAs) about
yourself, the people you know, the
world as you experience it, what is
right and wrong, good and bad.

Imagine exhaling all of that certainty
into a balloon. Now tie a string around
the balloon so the ABBAs don't seep out. Secure the end
of the string to yourself, perhaps through a belt loop. You
don't want your certainty floating away, after all. We want
it tethered to you, where you and others can see it, and
where you can pull it back in when you're ready.

But for now, leave it tied to you, floating quietly just
above your head.

You have just practiced suspending certainty.

Suspending certainty is suspending your belief in idea or
position...
> even your own ...
>> especially your own.

It is developing thinking for others to see.

It is suspending any need to be right or hold the correct answer, position or solution.

It is suspending all of your certainties and honestly holding them up for examination.

It is acknowledging that your truths are not everyone's truths and that truth is a moving target.

In the context of conversation, putting aside certainty is essential for learning to take place for certainty is the proverbial double-edged sword (meaning it will cut the learning no matter which edge is facing).

On the one edge, certainty, being right or needing to be right, is a learning disability.

If you are certain of your position you will not really hear the ideas of others. You may *appear* to be listening. You may even *think* you are listening; and yet you are not. You are judging what you are hearing as right (in agreement with you) or wrong (not in agreement with you) and deciding how to use what is being said to further your own position, because you already know the answer.

On the other edge, certainty spreads judgment and fear.

We will talk more about judgment and fear later on, but for now, keep in mind that your certainty can be felt by others, whether you openly state it or not. People can feel when they are being judged, so they shut down out of fear of being judged and or being found inadequate or incompetent. Thus, important ideas go unsaid and learning cannot advance beyond what is already held as certain.

The philosopher John Stuart Mill wrote that all ideas, even those most dearly held, must be questioned. There can be no certainties that are off-limits. Even if what is believed to be so is merely upheld upon examination, the very practice of examining our beliefs yields great learning. It reaffirms why we hold our beliefs, allows opportunities for us to adjust our beliefs to fit new information, and allows opportunities to teach those who were not present when the belief was formed.

Practicing suspending certainty will allow you to become more comfortable with your beliefs—as you more deeply understand why you hold them—and at the same time allow you to become more able to let them go when necessary—as you realize that they are based on the best information available at any given moment.

Practicing this discipline means accepting that making mistakes is part of learning. In fact, making mistakes is *critical* to learning. Think back to a significant learning moment in your life. Chances are it occurred because you (or someone close to you) screwed up.

4.   Hold space for difference

Facts which at first seem improbable will, even on scant explanation, drop the cloak of which has hidden them and stand forth in naked and simple beauty. (Galileo)

Conflict seems frightening to many of us, as we tend to dredge up memories of pain and humiliation, of being on the losing end. If managed poorly, conflict really is a frightening thing. It usually degenerates into personal attacks and vendettas, into competitions in which some win and others lose, into taking sides and plotting strategies. How many staff meetings or family discussions have you sat through in which someone raised their voice or stormed out of  the room spouting threats of getting even?

We often have difficulty embracing conflict because we are taught that it is a bad thing, something to be avoided.

So when we are faced with it, we tend to avoid it or ignore it. (I actually knew a CEO who firmly believed that if you ignored a problem long enough, it would go away.) If we can't avoid or ignore it, we often overreact because we feel cornered and forced into dealing with it.

And yet, if responded to effectively, conflict is a wonderful thing for it represents our uniqueness as individuals and leads to deeper and expanded understanding. It is proof that there are as many ways of thinking and doing as there are people. None of us has identical physical construction and experiences, and no one way is better, or more right, than another.

Holding space for difference in our conversations allows us to respectfully acknowledge all voices, to seek new ideas, to hear from those who might not otherwise speak, to look for ideas that oppose our own with the intent of learning how we can be, think, and do differently.

Holding space for difference is embracing differing points of view as opportunities for learning.

It is replacing the use of the word "but" with the word "and"
> because we realize that "but" negates everything that went before it.
>> (As in, "That's a good idea, but…")

It is noticing others who are silent and providing opportunity for involvement,
> while respecting those who choose not to speak.

It is deeply believing in the usefulness of other points of view.

It is being involved while being detached and
> open to outcomes that may not be your
> outcomes.

It is avoiding becoming fixated on one outcome or idea as the 'right' one.

As you practice holding space for difference you will notice a richness to your thinking and conversations, a level of creativity that perhaps you had not previously experienced. You will be more open to the ideas of others and, as a result, will find more ideas being shared with you. What you may have experienced as patience or tolerance will grow to a deeper respect for, and interest in, the ideas of others.

5.   Slow the conversation

Discovery follows discovery; each both raising and answering questions; each ending a long search, and each providing the new instruments for a new search. (J. Robert Oppenheimer)

Proceeding through our conversations with the deliberate intent of generating learning, listening deeply to others, and seeking diverse ideas all take time (which we tell ourselves we have too little of) and space (which we are often not comfortable allowing).

Think back to that time when you were deeply heard, and reflect on the pace of the conversation. It probably was slow, as you took time to choose words that would have the most meaning, as you allowed time for  the person listening to take in your words. You probably did not force conversation and were comfortable with silences. You probably allowed the conversation to follow its own course. You probably felt free to say what was on your heart, and wanted nothing less from the person listening.

This is what it feels like when we slow our conversations, and while it may seem uncomfortable when you first begin practicing, you will soon notice that it becomes habitual. Once you begin to make the space to reflect during your conversations, you will wonder how you ever managed to get by before.

Slowing the conversation means enabling silence in order to digest the previous speaker's words.

It means acknowledging other people's thoughts and ideas as significant.

It means taking time to reflect on how the words of others resonate with you and giving voice to that reaction.

It means taking time for the conversation to develop and deepen.

It means embracing silence as a way to deepen common understanding.

6. Voices

We must dare to think "unthinkable" thoughts.
We must learn to explore all the options and
possibilities that confront us in a complex and
rapidly changing world. We must learn to
welcome and not to fear the voices of dissent.
We must dare to think about "unthinkable things"
because when things become unthinkable,
thinking stops and action becomes mindless.
(J. William Fulbright)

How many times have we heard great ideas in parking lot meetings or water cooler conversations that did not arise in formal meetings?

Each of us speaks with a different voice that is reflective of our personal experiences. Age, gender, race, ethnicity, nationality, and status all influence how we perceive and describe the world, how we interact in it, what values or priorities we hold, which friends we choose, which books we read…every choice we make. And because we are all different, it is important that we all have the opportunity to have our voices heard.

You may object,
"Too many
voices, too many
ideas, and we
have chaos."

Or, "We really need to hear from *everyone!*"

Or, whisper to the person sitting next to you, "We all know that not everyone has good ideas."

And sure, we have all sat through meetings or presentations where we were thinking, "Why do I have to listen to this?" when the person was speaking about something we thought was utterly boring or completely irrelevant to us.

Every time we hear that voice in our heads or coming from our colleagues, what we are hearing is

the voice of judgment,

the voice that is saying it already knows the answer and so does not need to hear anything new,

the voice that is saying that ideas that come from someone who is younger or older, richer or poorer, of a different color or religion are somehow inferior.

Paula Underwood retold a Native American story entitled "Who Speaks for Wolf." Wolf represented the natural environment, and he was represented in the tribe by one member known as Wolf's Brother. During one council meeting, Wolf's Brother was not present to speak for Wolf, and a decision was made that caused great misfortune. The lesson, however, was learned. And afterward, the question was always asked at the tribal gatherings, "Who speaks for Wolf?" For Wolf was the one who wondered what might be true of circumstances that were yet unseen, what consequences would follow until the children and the children's children, what might have been forgotten in the discussion.

The power of a Learning Conversation is that every voice has the opportunity to be heard. A Learning Conversation creates meaning for everyone.

You now can accept that diversity in thinking strengthens systems because…

there is no single right way to accomplish a result.

We are all unique individuals, with unique insights and perspectives, and are capable of taking part in creating knowledge.

And remember that taking part in a Learning Conversation means that every participant is responsible for ensuring that the conversation yields the desired results. Should the conversation move off-topic, each person can ask whether this is the group's will. Should one person hijack the conversation to tell the story about their dear, departed Uncle Fred (again), each person can remind the group of their shared purpose.

Using the Learning Conversation Guidelines will keep a Learning Conversation flowing, will allow for varying levels of energy and interest on the part of the participants, will permit the conversation to progress naturally, along whatever path is most comfortable for the group, and will provide sufficient structure to ensure that the conversation outcomes are met.

7.   Synergy = Creativity²

Our lives are like islands in the sea, or like trees in the forest, which commingle their roots in the darkness underground. (William James)

Many and diverse voices are important because we are more creative collectively than alone. We have just forgotten how to work together because so many of our collective efforts—meetings, committee, teams—fail to achieve their potential and produce results.

Reflect on a time when you were part of a group that was "in the zone," when everything seemed to go right, when you seemed under the spell of some unstoppable force. Remember how that felt?

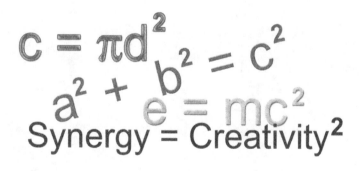

Most of us have had those experiences at one time or another, on a sports team or perhaps on a collaborative project, and we wish we could have more. Yet we approach those experiences as if they were the will of some higher power, a fluke, or fate, and assume they are beyond our control. But what if you were told that you can create that synergy whenever you want, with any group?

Well, you can. And the tools to do it have already been covered. Hold conversations that have a purpose. Teach the Learning Conversation Guidelines to your group, and practice them diligently, both individually and together.

Conversations build relationships.

Learning conversations build quality relationships.

Quality relationships lead you to shared vision, purpose and values.

Shared vision, purpose and values create alignment among individuals, so their energies are focused on desired outcomes and magnified in their intensity.

8. Tell your stories

And in that line now was a whiskered old man, with a linen cap and a crooked nose, who waited in a place called the Stardust Band Shell to share his part of the secret of heaven: that each affects the other and the other affects the next, and the world is full of stories, but the stories are all one. (Mitch Albom, The Five People You Meet in Heaven*)*

Telling stories and listening to them is universal, found in every culture, and to such an extent that it is part of how we process the world around us. Telling and listening to stories is how we share information, how we teach and how we learn. It is how we create and instill cultural values

long, long ago,
in a land far away...

IT WAS A DARK AND STORMY NIGHT...

Once upon a time...

I REMEMBER...

and norms. It is how we affirm our identity and our role in society. It is how we practice social interaction, making up stories, acting them out and playing different roles.

Storytelling is important as it allows storytellers to share collective wisdom and transfer culture from one generation to another. And this is true of any society or any organization. Think about all of the "war stories" you have listened to or told—stories about how things used to be, who did what, what great things were accomplished or what horrendous mistakes were made. We remember those stories because they trigger an emotional response in us. We identify with one of the characters or emotions described. And we carry the lessons with us, much longer than any fact memorized from a textbook.

Part of holding a Learning Conversation is sharing stories and we all have stories to tell. The key to using stories is to pick the right one and to tell it authentically.

Know who you are as a storyteller…

> know yourself physically and be comfortable in your body;

> know the voice from which you speak;

> know yourself spiritually, deeply, as this will give you vitality as a storyteller.

Talk in metaphors, dreams, archetypal images and emotional experiences,

> rather than reciting linear sequences of facts.

Pick a story that has influence and impact…

Influence is energy created by the intersection of ourselves and others.

Impact is the residual change in people after you have left them.

Know why you are telling the story...
Remember, stories are a means of teaching.

So how are you trying to shift someone's thinking?

Know your listener...
And reach out to both head and heart. Make your listener a character in your story.

Know what legacy you want to leave in their hearts.

And remember, the gift you give as a storyteller is the gift of helping people see beyond themselves.

9. Words matter

Words hang like wash on the line, blowing in the winds of the mind. (Rameshwar Das)

The difference between the right word and the almost right word is the difference between lightning and a lightning bug. (Mark Twain)

Because they are so powerful, words must be chosen carefully. Words are much more than letters strung together. They are the means by which we convey our thoughts to one another.

Words touch all of our senses. They have a rhythm we can feel and hear. They evoke pictures in our minds. They help us recall memories, sights, smells, and experiences.

Like most other disciplines, leadership has its own language—and to communicate as a leader is to speak in that language.

Much of the traditional language of leadership has relied on metaphors from sports or the military. Motivational speeches are a way to "rally the troops," making a good sale is "hitting a home run."

These metaphors call up for us very specific mental images, whether we are conscious of them or not. These images create a certain worldview, one that reinforces the industrial-military mindset.

The new edge of leadership seeks to create a different worldview, one that achieves results through cooperation and caring.

And to speak the new language of leadership means choosing words that reflect a connection to other people and to the earth—organic words and metaphors rather than mechanistic ones. For example, the new language of leadership uses words like "grow" rather than "build" and would compare team development to cultivating a garden rather than winning a game.

This organic language changes our mental images, which, in turn, changes our worldview to one of connectedness.

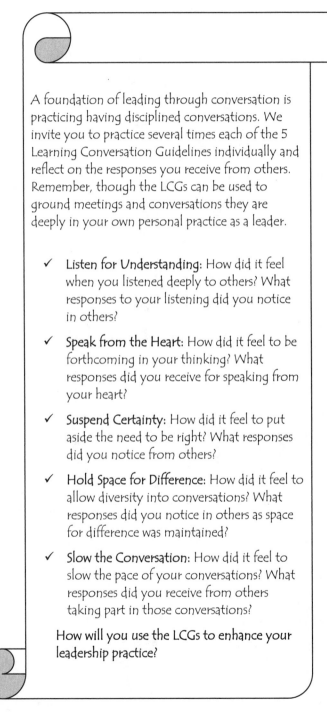

A foundation of leading through conversation is practicing having disciplined conversations. We invite you to practice several times each of the 5 Learning Conversation Guidelines individually and reflect on the responses you receive from others. Remember, though the LCGs can be used to ground meetings and conversations they are deeply in your own personal practice as a leader.

✓ **Listen for Understanding:** How did it feel when you listened deeply to others? What responses to your listening did you notice in others?

✓ **Speak from the Heart:** How did it feel to be forthcoming in your thinking? What responses did you receive for speaking from your heart?

✓ **Suspend Certainty:** How did it feel to put aside the need to be right? What responses did you notice from others?

✓ **Hold Space for Difference:** How did it feel to allow diversity into conversations? What responses did you notice in others as space for difference was maintained?

✓ **Slow the Conversation:** How did it feel to slow the pace of your conversations? What responses did you receive from others taking part in those conversations?

How will you use the LCGs to enhance your leadership practice?

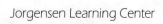

PART TWO:
LEADERS AND LEARNERS,
OH MY

*or why leaders learn
and learners lead*

10. Learning is leading

*In times of change, learners inherit the Earth,
while the learned find themselves beautifully
equipped to deal with a world that no longer
exists. (Eric Hoffer)*

Learning is the key to remaining adaptable and flexible in times of change; those who are bound by certainty eventually become obsolete. Leaders should be those who remain ahead of the tides of change; they should, by definition, be learners. Leaders should raise others to be adaptable and flexible, so they must encourage learning in those whom they lead.

Now, to give this discussion a few more twists…

Leaders are at their best when they are learning, not when they are teaching. It would seem natural, especially in our culture, to revere the wise leader who knows all.

The problem with this, however, is that it is a myth. Leaders cannot know all—not about their organization, their industry, their environment, or their people. When leaders think they know all, they become trapped in certainty and risk becoming obsolete. When those who follow them think the leaders know all, they risk stifling their own creativity by limiting their knowledge to that of their leaders.

As was pointed out earlier, diversity in ideas is a powerful and natural resource for any organization. Why would any leader limit the creation and sharing of ideas for the sake of being right?

Leadership is not having all of the answers. Leadership is not teaching one set of ideas.

Further, remember the old saying about leaders being born and not made? Well, from our perspective, leaders are *not* born. They do not have some magic quality that distinguishes them from the rest of humanity. Leaders are made, and they are made from the sum of their learning experiences. The more they learn, the better the quality of their leadership. The more they remain learners, the more the quality of their leadership will continue to improve.

By being in a position of learning, **leaders are consistently open to the ideas of others, less concerned with the need to be right or to bear all responsibility, and less focused on creating a world in their image.** They become more intent on nurturing the organizations they lead and on growing the potential of the individuals in their care. In our judgment, a litmus test for leaders is to answer the question: Are the lives of the people that we lead improved professionally and personally over time?

11. Container of learning

Here's to the crazy ones, the misfits, the rebels, the troublemakers, the round pegs in the square holes... the ones who see things differently -- they're not fond of rules... You can quote them, disagree with them, glorify or vilify them, but the only thing you can't do is ignore them because they change things... they push the human race forward, and while some may see them as the crazy ones, we see genius, because the ones who are crazy enough to think that they can change the world, are the ones who do. (Steve Jobs)

So we see that leadership is largely about cultivating the ideas of others, of creating the garden and letting others plant and reap. Leaders define the boundaries by putting a fence around the garden. They create the conditions for sustaining creativity by providing resources—the equivalent of food, water, sunlight in the garden. And they let those in the garden do what they do best—grow ideas and make things happen.

Or, to use a different metaphor, **leaders create and hold a container of learning. They hold a space open, and they do this by embracing learning as well as by teaching and learning through disciplined conversations.**

Leaders do not hold the people in the space. Doing so would not serve the interests of the individual or the organization. People who are held and supported by leadership do not thrive, they do not create, and become dependent on that support. They keep people in what Piaget termed a parent/child relationship, with the leader telling people what to do and how best to do it, much like a parent guides a child.

Instead, leaders give people the space to learn and create and then set them free. Leaders continually reinforce why things should be done, but they do not dictate <u>what</u> should be done or <u>how</u>.

This is a valuable opportunity for leaders to do what they do best: to go forth and show the way.

12. Mental models

The eye sees a great many things, but the average brain records very few of them. (Thomas Edison)

Mental models are our personal understandings of the world according to us; these models contain the attitudes, beliefs and assumptions that shape our daily actions. They govern our ideas of how things should work, how things are, and how things should or could be. These convictions form the basis of our personal and organizational thinking structure.

Examples of mental models are:

All men are created equal.

We simply have an unlimited supply of resources and can throw away our waste.

Mental models are often very hard to surface (which is what we do when we practice suspending certainty) because they...

are incomplete and constantly evolving;

can contain errors and contradictions;

are sometimes buried deep in our subconscious;

are overly simplified explanations of a complex world.

The discipline of working with mental models starts with turning the mirror inward—learning to unearth our internal pictures of the world, to bring them to the surface and hold them rigorously to scrutiny. It also includes the ability to carry on Learning Conversations that balance inquiry and advocacy, where people expose their own thinking effectively and make that thinking open to the influence of others.

When someone is speaking with certainty, they are not just giving their opinion, they are providing you insight into the way they view the world.

If you can shift how someone thinks by shifting their mental models, then you will change the way they act.

So we see that, ultimately, leaders nurture quality relationships through quality conversations.

Learning takes place in quality conversations. As learning takes place, thinking shifts. And as thinking shifts, behavior shifts.

Mental models are our personal understandings of the world according to us; these models contain the attitudes, beliefs and assumptions that shape our daily actions. They are our personal maps (and the map is never the territory). They govern our ideas of how things should work, how things are, and how things should or could be. These convictions form the basis of our personal and organizational thinking structure.

If you are going to attempt to shift someone's mental models, be prepared.

Encountering new ideas, methods, beliefs, and processes makes people feel unsettled because they push the boundaries of their comfort zone. This is why the first tendency in dealing with change is to resist—our mental models anchor our identity within a system of beliefs. We define ourselves in terms of the sum of our beliefs, and we defend our positions because we feel as if our self-worth is at stake.

There is also the risk of falling into the trap of wanting something for someone else, even if what you want seems (to you) to be good for them. Wanting something for someone else places you in the position of judging, and possibly trying to control, what someone else thinks, says, or does, and keeps the relationship from developing. (We say more about this a little later).

And finally, in attempting to shift someone else's thinking, you may end up changing your own. If you are resistant to change, if you feel that you are right, or your idea is best, this can be tricky to see, much less deal with.

But once you shift someone's mental models (even your own), by creating conditions that allow them to interact with the world differently and by supporting their positive self-talk, they will be able to create whatever they desire. Channel that desire toward the shared vision, and stand back.

13. Talking to yourself

Man is made by his belief. As he believes, so he is. (Bhagavad Gita)

A man is as happy as he makes up his mind to be. (Abraham Lincoln)

The power in understanding mental models is that once you do, you will hold the key to unlimited creativity. So we are going to spend some time digging a little deeper into our minds to see how our self-talk, what we tell ourselves

(No, you are not the only person who talks to yourself)

shapes our mental models.

Your subconscious mind is the storage compartment of the mind, where we keep and process events, feelings, beliefs, opinions, truths and expectations. The processes of our circulatory, digestive, and breathing systems are controlled automatically by the subconscious.

Here comes the really cool part...

The subconscious mind operates on *beliefs*. It will accept any suggestion and respond according to the nature of that suggestion. It makes no distinction between good and bad, truth and fiction. Once our subconscious mind accepts an idea, it begins to put it into action. To the subconscious mind, our thoughts are realities.

Your ability to create lies within your mind—the part called the Creative Subconscious Mind—which has only one function: *to ensure your truths come true.*

The creative subconscious picks up the images or words that you generate through your conscious mind and begins creating what it sees. Your subconscious mind only ever says 'YES' to what your conscious mind says to it.

Through a process of
continual
reinforcement, your
truths become your
reality and make up
who you are and
how you see the

world. Your subconscious mind then establishes very firm
boundaries around your truths and protects them, which
gives continuity to your mental models so you can
function from one moment to the next. In short, it
creates and secures your comfort zone.

14. Mirror, mirror

There are two ways of spreading light: to be the candle or the mirror that reflects it. (Edith Wharton)

Beauty is eternity gazing at itself in the mirror. But you are eternity and you are the mirror. (Khalil Gibran)

Behavior is the mirror in which everyone shows their image. (Goethe)

There is an old adage about looking in the mirror before you look out the window, advising us to first search our own hearts before looking to the world around us for answers or reasons. This practice of looking inward, of reflection, is an important one for leaders.

Leaders lead living systems, systems that are in constant states of flux. If you do not take time to pause momentarily—to think about what has been and what is now and to dream of what can be—you may find yourself getting lost in the demands of daily life. Reflection can help you see the bigger picture, rather than events in slices of time. Reflection can help you understand the connection between past and present, to see how the consequences of past decisions are tied to what is happening around you now. Reflection gives you the space to see the interconnectedness that provides the structure of any living system.

More deeply, **reflection can help you remain attuned to who you are.** In difficult times in life (when we are confused and disheartened as well as times of exhilaration when life is filled with joy and happiness) taking time to reflect helps you center yourself and provides room for learning.

As you begin regularly taking time to reflect,
> to journal or meditate or use whatever reflective practice you are comfortable with,

you may find that the thoughts that emerge during this time are stepping stones to a deeper understanding of the patterns you see in your leadership practice. Remember: patterns are not random. When thoughts keep appearing, that is your cue to look for the underlying mental models and structures that are causing the pattern. By following these trails of thoughts, you will find yourself drawn more strongly to your authentic self, the part of you that must show up if you are to lead and engage others effectively.

"So I get that reflection is important," you say. And probably like you did when we discussed the Learning Conversation Guideline of slowing down our conversations, you also say, "I don't have time to stop and just think." Yes, it happens that sometimes the time and space set aside for reflection gets lost in the process of leading. As with any discipline, it is partly a matter of finding a habit that works best for you—early morning, late night, middle of the day…it does not matter. When you notice that you've stopped,

commit to taking a few minutes that day. It's just that simple. Once the discipline of reflection has become internalized, it will simply become part of your life, one that adds immeasurably to your sense of self, the clarity of your thinking, and the quality of your interactions with others.

If we play with this image of a mirror, then it is easy to see how we must be our own mirrors, that we must be able to look into ourselves and see ourselves looking back at us.

And yet we are also the mirror to others, often reflecting what we see and feel around us. To see this capacity you have to be a mirror, begin to pay attention to yourself during different interactions during your day. If others around you are tense, do you also become tense? If others are happy, do you also feel happy? This tendency to mimic our environment is a survival skill passed down from the earliest human beings. Empathy, after all, is a bond which connects all humans, and empathy derives from mirror neurons in the brain—neurons that allow us to interpret and imitate the feelings of others. It is so intuitive that often we slip into a mirror role without realizing it. When we do learn to recognize this ability, we can guide it so that we reflect what we *want* to see or feel rather than what we *do* see or feel.

Reflecting both inwardly and outwardly is a capability that takes practice. It empowers leaders in both their personal life and in their role as dreamer and visionary. Deep reflection enables leaders to refine the necessary action they must take to maintain aspiration in the system.

Jorgensen Learning Center

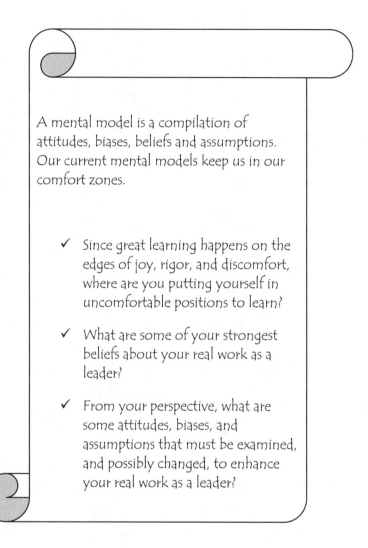

A mental model is a compilation of attitudes, biases, beliefs and assumptions. Our current mental models keep us in our comfort zones.

✓ Since great learning happens on the edges of joy, rigor, and discomfort, where are you putting yourself in uncomfortable positions to learn?

✓ What are some of your strongest beliefs about your real work as a leader?

✓ From your perspective, what are some attitudes, biases, and assumptions that must be examined, and possibly changed, to enhance your real work as a leader?

PART THREE:
TAPPING INTO THE SPIRIT
OF LEADING

15.   Linear approaches don't work in a loopy world

Individuality is only possible if it unfolds from wholeness. (David Bohm)

Though people love lists and steps, lists and steps are not helpful for dealing with the complexities of life. The world doesn't move in a linear manner. So forcing our work into a linear form can limit our success.

The world is comprised of interrelated and interdependent systems. A system is a collection of individual elements that come together to fulfill some shared purpose. Systems exist all around: environmental systems or telecommunications systems, as well families, teams, societies, political  parties, and our organizations. Philosophical and scientific theories or organizational visions are systems. Even our bodies are systems.

To see the world in its systems form is to be a systems thinker. Systems thinking is a language that enables us to see the whole, to see our organizations, our lives, our world, as a series of inter-connected, interdependent systems, each comprised of a multitude of interconnected, interdependent subsystems. So our work, and our lives, are loopy, not linear…messy, not neat. Lists and steps are great tools to help folks practice specific tasks, like grocery shopping or assembling a bike. Although important in accomplishing daily projects, lists and steps do not help us see the whole. Systems cannot be moved following a set series of steps, and the people within the systems do not function sequentially, either. Sometimes, to achieve your desired results, you have to start at step 3, then go to step 1, then maybe loop around to step 7. Linear thinking does not allow for this.

Systems thinking allows leaders to see the flow and their place in, and influence over, the flow. Systems are dynamic; they are always in a state of ebb and flow, growth and diminishment. Change and adaptability, therefore, are constant and must be everpresent factors in decision making.

Systems thinking helps leaders develop a long-term approach with a focus on sustainability, and as such it requires a long-range mindset.

Systems thinking helps leaders maintain an open mindset because the plurality of voices in the system must be heard to keep the systems pictures clear.

Systems thinking allows interested parties to work *on* the system, and it allows everyone to recognize how they fit *in* the system.

Below are a few systems assumptions to keep us on the leadership path:

Systems Assumption: Most issues that are faced in the present are the result of decisions, actions, and solutions from the past. We are the custodians of other people's designs, just as those who come after us will be the custodians of our designs.

Systems Assumption: Typically, cause and effect do not live next to each other; they are often separated in time and space, and a linear approach would not allow us to weave through the complexity to find the connection. As an example, a decision to bury a hazardous material may not have an impact on the environment until years later, and that effect may not appear at the burial site, but in another ecosystem located far away.

To carry this thought a bit further: all actions have side effects, intended and unintended...anticipated and unanticipated.

Systems Assumption: Systems thinking shows us that patterns in our systems are not random. They are caused by structures that support the systems. Structures include such things as policies, procedures, rules, laws, requirements, expectations, hierarchies, organizational charts, job descriptions.

Structures are designed according to someone's mental models of what should be done and how it should be done; they are designed to produce a certain end. If you  are not getting the results that you want, chances are this is because the structures in place are not permitting you to do what you need to do. To change the structures requires that you define the structures and the mental models that created them.

Systems Assumption: Elimination is a normal living systems function. Systems are always striving to achieve homeostasis, so if you include something in your system of work and do not remove something else, your system will become cluttered and inefficient.

Imagine that you are feeling stressed. You decide you would like to take a yoga class to help reduce stress. If you do not give up something else, then the yoga class becomes one more thing added into an already busy life (otherwise, you wouldn't be stressed, right?).

So you may attend the yoga class diligently for awhile, but eventually it will begin to feel like a burden…you will attend less and less…then you will feel guilty about not attending…and your self-talk will spiral around thoughts like "I can't keep up" or "I'm so overwhelmed" or "That's money down the drain"…and then you find yourself stressed over the yoga class that was supposed to relieve your stress.

The same holds true around your work, as well. It is hard to say "No," and yet it is one of the best ways to maintain balance in the system. Say "No" to projects you do not really want to work on. When you can't say "No"—and we've all had *those* projects—then reprioritize your other work and let something else slide while you work on what you have to work on.

16. Dare to dream

You must give birth to your images.
They are the future waiting to be born.
Fear not the strangeness that you feel.
The future must enter you long before it
happens.

Just wait for the birth, for the hour of new clarity.
(Ranier Maria Rilke)

The real work of leaders—the single most important thing a leader does—is create and hold a dream, a vision of what the world, or some part of it, will be in the future. Once this picture is developed and articulated, leaders enroll others by matching personal visions of success with the enterprise vision or dream to create common aspiration.

Leaders share that dream daily with people so they can help make it happen by recognizing how accomplishing their personal vision supports the enterprise dream.

Leaders believe in the people who are working to make it happen.

Dreams give you purpose, something to aspire to. They are the outlet for your creative mind. They allow you to see what can be, without any limitations, and provide the

desire to see the dream become reality for both the individual and the organization.

Otto Scharmer of the Presencing Institute beautifully described the power of dreams in his book, *Theory U.* Dreams have the power to take hold of us, to compel us forward at all levels—consciously, subconsciously, and unconsciously. Once we have enrolled in a dream, it becomes something that we must do; in fact, we can't *not* do it.

Without the capacity to suspend the voices of judgment, fear and cynicism, we would not find what Scharmer called the "place of most potential." We discipline ourselves to suspend, to change the habits of the past, so that we can enter a "new place of inquiry and wonder."

An edge to this description of dreams that must be surfaced is that in order to change, in order to have and hold the dream, we must willingly let go of our old selves in order to give birth to the new. We must surrender to the future as it comes towards us.

17. Creative tension, not stress

I am always doing that which I cannot do, in order that I may learn how to do it. (Pablo Picasso)

Sharing the dream and getting others to enroll in it requires creating the space for creativity. This space comes from the chaos of our interdependent, interconnected world of systems. It is shaped by following the Learning Conversation Guidelines. It is a dark and scary space that finds light in the sharing of the dream.

Leaders create the conditions which are conducive to creative life, and often this means putting aside the traditional productivity drivers or measures.

Leaders must connect with the people around them and align each person's dreams with the shared dream.

Leaders focused on aspiration hold conversations around the ways that individuals contribute daily to accomplishing the shared dream. They should encourage the people around them to expand their learning so they can sustain their work toward the shared dream.

Leaders should not seek to motivate individuals because they can't motivate other people. Instead, leaders can create an environment in which individuals motivate themselves.

Leaders are able, in this context, to allow people to stretch their abilities, to learn and grow. When the desire to accomplish a dream is shared, each person can then decide what they need to learn in order to best contribute.

This continual learning in order to better contribute to the shared dream is the state of creative tension…

> in which each individual feels just enough pull to learn and grow,

>> but not so much pull that the tension becomes stress.

18. Visualize relationships the way you want them to be

No pessimist ever discovered the secrets of the stars, or sailed an uncharted land, or opened a new heaven to the human spirit. (Helen Keller)

If you do want a relationship, one way to create it is to imagine the relationship (your interactions with that person on all levels) as you wish them to be and aspire to create that relationship. Be careful that the relationship you aspire to is truly the one you want. It is easy to fall into the trap of wanting something for the other person, and we'll address that a bit later.

Once you have visualized the relationship as you want it to be, write down this aspiration and act as if it is already a reality. The change in your actions will naturally shift the other person's reactions.

Chances are, if there is someone around you who you do not like or respect, you do not have a good relationship with them and you are not leading them as effectively as you could.

If you have such people around you, you must first decide whether you want a relationship with them. If you do *not*, it is best to have a heartfelt conversation to severe the relationship, be it personal or professional.

If you *do* want a relationship, one way to create it is to imagine the relationship (your interactions with that person on all levels) as you wish them to be. Be careful that the relationship you are imagining is healthy for both of you and is attainable. It is easy to fall into the trap of wanting something for the other person, and we'll address that a bit later.

Once you have visualized the relationship as you want it to be, act as if it is already a reality. The change in your actions will naturally shift the other person's reactions.

Be mindful that the relationship will not change overnight, especially if you have a long history with the other person. It will take time to rebuild the trust. In the meantime, you will need to sustain the image of the new relationship and remain consistent in your new actions.

19.   One thing

Your work is to discover your work and then with all your heart to give yourself to it. (Buddha)

Trying to do too much with limited time seems to be a pattern of behavior prevalent in all aspects of life today. The solution to this dilemma is really quite simple and yet to say it out loud invariably elicits eye rolls or looks of outright shock.

The solution is to do less. **Focus on fewer things and do them well.** In the book *Good to Great* by Jim Collins, this is described as the hedgehog concept.

In Buddhist thinking, it is embodied in the principle of doing only one thing at a time.

In fact, the human brain can process multiple inputs, but to do so it must operate according to set methods. When the brain takes in information from multiple sources simultaneously, it files those inputs together in memory. This is why the smell of pizza reminds you of your vacation in Italy and why you can find your lost keys by retracing your steps.

In most situations, this is not a problem. But what happens when your child studies for a test while listening to her favorite song (over and over and over)? Or what happens when you rehearse your big sales presentation in your office and have to present it in the client's office?

There are two lessons to be shared. First, learning is contextual so to ensure that you are teaching and learning effectively use different settings, different methods, talk with different people and vary the time of day you talk with them. Even taking a different route to the office can shift your perspective.

Second, multi-tasking is a myth. We can only really do one thing at a time well. By doing only one thing at a time, that one thing has your full attention—body, mind and soul. When you are talking to someone, on the phone or in person, focus solely on the conversation. When you are eating, focus only on the food.

It may seem as if this approach will slow things down and lower productivity. And it may indeed lower the volume of things you do. But it will greatly increase the quality of what you do and reduce those annoying unintended consequences that emanate from things to which we do not give full attention. And as a leader, slowing down will help you cultivate higher quality relationships with those around you and with yourself.

Find a pattern that lives in your system which you enjoy and which gives you good results. Reflect on the designs that support that system and write them down.

Find a system that lives in your system which you would like to change. Reflect on the designs which support that system and write them down. What can you as a leader do to influence a change in that pattern?

What do you do to keep creative tension alive for your own development?

We are in a trusting relationship when we are forthcoming with our thinking. High quality relationships generate this kind of operational trust.

✓ Identify some relationships you have with others that are outstanding from your perspective as a leader. How will you use Conversational Leadership techniques to further and deepen these relationships?

✓ Conversely, identify a professional relationship that needs attention or even repair. Regardless of how this relationship came to be in its current reality, please try the following three-step process repeatedly:

   o Visualize the relationship the way you want it to be.
   o Describe this relationship in writing as though the new relationship has already occurred, using first-person, present-tense, future-focused writing.
   o Behave as though this relationship is already the way you wish it to be.

✓ Once you have attempted this process, journal about the response from the other person with whom you do not have a quality relationship. Reflect on how it felt to carry out these steps and the changes you notice in the relationship over time.

PART FOUR:
THOUGHTS TO PONDER
ON YOUR JOURNEY

The points offered for your consideration are based on the feedback from leaders of all sizes, shapes, styles, and beliefs in their daily practice. This feedback is filtered through the lens of Peter Senge's three leadership capabilities: aspiration, effective conversation, and seeing the whole. These points reflect our best understanding of the collective wisdom of people we have worked with.

20. The only way out is through

In the middle of difficulty lies opportunity. (Albert Einstein)

When life becomes difficult, when there are issues that we rather not face, when there are just too many demands, people face the urge to withdraw or ignore what they don't want to deal with.

This approach may work in the short term. But it doesn't work forever. Avoidance only compounds problems.

The only way out of difficult times is to face situations with honesty and without judgment of yourself or others…

Remind yourself of your dream…

Reorient yourself and move forward…

Use the Learning Conversation Guidelines…

Nurture necessary conversations…

Always close the loop.

21. Many a truth is said in jest

Sarcasm helps keep you from telling people what you really think of them. (Anonymous)

Humor is one of the ways that human beings cope with the world. Humor lets us communicate our amusement at things that are funny. And it lets us cope with emotionally stressful situations, with confusion, with frustration, with sadness.

Humor is also a way of communicating things we are not comfortable saying directly. We make light of serious situations; we use sarcasm to say one thing on the surface, and something else at a deeper level.

We tease others when they step outside the boundaries, when they make a mistake, or do something embarrassing.

Teasing and sarcasm in some contexts are often used as a means of control, to force others to conform to what we want or think is right.

This is not to say that humor should be avoided or that leaders can't crack jokes. It is simply a reminder to be clear about what is being communicated. If a performance issue needs to be addressed, saying "Great job, Bob" while wink-winking during a staff meeting is not the best way to do it. It is better to speak directly if there is a question or concern rather than disguise what you want to say behind a mask of humor.

22.   Addictions come in many shapes and sizes

Every form of addiction is bad, no matter whether the narcotic be alcohol, morphine or idealism. (Carl Jung)

The word addiction usually conjures up images of alcohol, drugs, gambling, shopping, eating, and other publicized activities.

There are many, many other types of addiction, and some are so deeply rooted within us that we don't even realize we are caught in an addictive cycle. **Addictions are ways that people learn to cope with the world, to gain control or to attempt to create a sense of self and place.**

Unless we learn to recognize addictive behaviors, we will not be able to work through them.

This is harder than it would appear because many times what people are addicted to are not external objects, but to other people or types of people, and to certain behaviors.

If we understand that addiction occurs between a person and something outside that person, we can see addictive behaviors in the repeating patterns within that person's personal or work life.

Sometimes this requires taking a step back because the pattern is found in various relationships, not in a specific object or type of object.

And sometimes people behave in a certain way because they have learned that those actions almost invariably generate a desired reaction from others. Ever had a friend or colleague who lied about accomplishments to get praise? That's an addictive behavior, with the praise being the object of addiction. Ever had a colleague who created crises so they could solve them? That, too, is an addictive behavior.

In the practice of leadership, you do not have to become an expert in psychology, only a disciplined practitioner of systems thinking, aspiration, and effective conversations.

23. Nature abhors a vacuum

No one gossips about other people's secret virtues. (Bertrand Russell)

Wherever a void exists, people will naturally try to fill it in the best way they know how, in much the same way the brain fills in missing words in a sentence.

If there is a void in information, people will fill it with gossip, innuendo, speculations or projections of their own fears and desires. This filler is based on nostalgia and amnesia, or to use the phrase coined by Jaime Vollmer,

nostesia. Nostalgia shows up in our imaginings as a way of bringing the past back to life. If we don't know what is going on currently or what is going to happen in the near future, then we will leap to conclusions based on the past.

In crises, this usually looks something like: "Sales are down 20% right now. Last time when sales were down only 10%, 30 people got fired. No one is telling us anything because they're going to fire at least 60 people."

In our daily work, nostalgia explains why people keep doing what they've always done—often because they don't have a clear picture of where they're supposed to be going, so they relive the past for want of a vision of the future.

To compound nostalgia, we also get selective amnesia around the past, which means we remember our version of the past. So the past we are trying to recreate is quite possibly one that isn't shared by others, and very likely is one that never existed.

What gets plugged into the void then gets passed around as truth. And if you have ever played the telephone game, you know there is more distortion of the message the farther you get from the source, so that the original gossip or speculation most likely has become something different by the time it runs full course.

This is why leaders must remain consistent in their language and actions and be as transparent as they can. This is why the language of leadership should not be hidden in jokes, sarcasm, fear, avoidance or blame.

A way to stop gossip and rampant musings, once begun, is to provide accurate information and connect the accurate information to the shared dream or aspiration, so it can live and be shared with others in that context.

To prevent gossip from misaligning the system and causing people to lose energy and focus, it is necessary to continually check for common understanding around the shared dream, around the connection of daily work to the shared dream, around responsibilities and successes— aspiration can be in every conversation.

24. Spot the imposters

No snowflake ever falls in the wrong place.
(Zen saying)

Imposters lurk anywhere in the system that the desire for acceptance or validation lives. **An imposter is any form of judgment or evaluation that is not connected to aspasiration or tied to the shared dream and not based on results and evidence.**

Imposters come in all shapes and sizes; they could be people or structures in the system, such as training class evaluations or performance reviews.

These people and structures are imposters because they give a false report based on false criteria.

If you base a relationship on a shared dream…

> if you have shared understanding about what the dream is and how each individual;

> contributes to accomplishing the shared dream…

if you establish mutually agreed-upon results for each person's work...

if you establish the evidence that will be demonstrated if each person is doing

what they should be doing...

if you check daily, weekly, monthly with each person,

and have conversations with them about how their work helps move everyone toward the

shared dream,

and about whether evidence is being generated to show they are meeting results...

then you will have a way of evaluating your system that

is based on quality relationships

honors the contributions of each individual

sustains the shared dream

and generates evidence of success.

25. Balance

The best and safest thing is to keep a balance in your life, acknowledge the great powers around us and in us. If you can do that, and live that way, you are really a wise man. (Euripides)

Balance in the individual
between mind, body and spirit.

Balance in life
between work, others
and self.

Touch each element every
day.

Physical: Do something
physical every day to reconnect to your body. Dance.
Walk. Do yoga.

Professional: Do something to further your professional
dreams. Learn something new. Teach someone. Go to a
networking event. Write a paper.

Intellectual: Do something to stimulate your intellect.
Read. Take a class. Do a puzzle.

Emotional: Do something to care for your emotional
well-being. Watch a funny movie. Go to dinner with
someone you love.

Spiritual: Do something to care for your spiritual well-being. Meditate. Attend a service or ceremony. Pray.

Human beings are complex systems and balance comes when each aspect is individually cared for.

26. To everything there is a season

Live each season as it passes; breathe the air, drink the drink, taste the fruit, and resign yourself to the influences of each. (Henry David Thoreau)

Part of leadership is embracing flux. Things come and go, move into the system and move out. People are engaged sometimes, and not engaged other times; they move in and out of the system, in and out of phases of interest, in and out of assignments and responsibilities. Systems themselves are in constant motion; they come into being, serve their purpose, then die.

Immortality is achieved, not through continued preservation of what exists now, but through continued creation of something new. If you look at nature, species don't die out completely before they are replaced. Nature grows the new amidst what exists. It is a continual process. Human systems, as they can mirror this natural flow, should embrace the process of giving life to new ideas, new lines of business, even new ways of being while sustaining what currently exists as long (as it is healthy to do so).

27.   You can't want things for other people

The servant-leader is servant first. Becoming a servant-leader begins with the natural feeling that one wants to serve, to serve first. Then conscious choice brings one to aspire to lead. . . . The best test is this: Do those served grow as persons? Do they, while being served, become healthier, wiser, freer, more autonomous, more likely themselves to become servants? (Robert K. Greenleaf)

The best way to find yourself is to lose yourself in the service of others. (Ghandi)

I start with the premise that the function of leadership is to produce more leaders, not more followers. (Ralph Nader)

As leaders, we are conditioned to be caring, nurturing, sympathetic—in a word, parental. We are taught that we should seek to better those around us and we often find ourselves doing this by trying to fix or change the *person*, not the *system*.

Yet in our personal lives, with friends or family, most of us have come to realize that we can't fix or change people— in fact, many people do not *want* to be fixed or changed. It's odd that we think some measure of professional authority gives us this ability.

But employees are just like everyone else; they don't want to be fixed or changed. Wishing someone were more engaged, would take on new responsibility, or would not be a micro-manager are all examples of wanting something for someone else, wanting someone to be or do something other than what they are capable of.

This is not only unproductive, it suppresses aspiration… and it is dangerous. **Wanting something for someone else undermines any relationship you may have with that person. It shows you cannot accept them for who they are and probably cannot respect them or their ideas.** The success of any organization, any leadership model, rests on relationships. If you don't have a relationship with someone, you will not be able to lead them.

Remember, systems thinking teaches us that most problems are the result of the system, not the individual people. The people in the system are generally doing the best they can given the resources they have and their understanding of reality.

Much of leadership requires working on the system to design and redesign structures that generate the desired results. One characteristic of a living system is elimination; eliminating structures that prevent the system from moving towards the desired result is a necessary aspect of working on the system.

28. Followers

The easiest thing in the world to be is you. The most difficult thing to be is what other people want you to be. Don't let them put you in that position. (Leo Buscaglia)

The leadership principles we have been discussing are not linear, and so it stands to reason that the followers of systems thinking leaders are not linear in their followership.

Linear followership looks like ducklings following a duck, with each duckling in a line behind the parent duck. This model works for ducks because the leader, the parent, is responsible for the survival of the ducklings.

We have already said that the relationship between leaders and followers is not that of parent to child. Leaders create the conditions (the space) in which it is safe to play.

In this environment, **followers remain connected to the leader through the shared dream, but they have a wide circumference of action.** Sometimes followers roam ahead of the leader, sometimes to the side, and sometimes behind.

The leader's work is to create and sustain the vision, then steward those who are enrolled to accomplish their personal visions as they contribute to shared success.

29. The weakest link

The weakest link in the chain is also the strongest. It can break the chain. (Stanislaw Jerzy Lec)

Though we like to hold the most consistent performers as the exemplars of our systems, in practice it is **the worst performer who sets the standard for everyone else.**

The worst performer establishes the minimum level of acceptable performance for the system. This level of performance is the bar against which everyone else measures their own work.

As a leader, the lowest standard of performance you accept reflects your expectations of everyone.

Consistently poor performers weaken the system. Their very presence indicates that the system is not strong enough to protect itself from them.

30. Practicing a discipline is hard until it isn't

We do not walk on our legs, but on our Will.
(Sufi proverb)

This section is a reminder to you that the work involved in putting these principles into action is a discipline.

If you accept this model of leadership, you will find that internalizing the concepts takes conscious and sustained effort for a while. Remember, you are changing some of your mental models around what it means to be a leader. **Focus and discipline are the keys to your sustained success.**

The time it takes to internalize ideas and change habits and comfortable patterns varies individual to individual.

Your learning will go more quickly and your practice improve more rapidly if you have a partner or group to work with, even if that partner is someone outside your organization.

You are learning a new way of thinking, speaking, and being; think of this model as an immersion program for leaders. It is helpful to have someone who has the same experiences and speaks the same language to talk to, share ideas and questions with. But the simple fact remains: practice, practice, practice is what it takes.

31.   Is that a mouse in your pocket?

The only people who should use the Royal We are editors and people with tapeworms. (Mark Twain)

To make ideas more palatable or to gain support, we often defer to someone else's expertise or speak as if we are the representative of a group. This can be dangerous if you do not really represent a group or if you misspeak on behalf of someone else.

Conversation is most meaningful when we show up as ourselves and share only our thoughts and ideas. Urging others to rally around our ideas, or stating ideas as if they belong to many others misrepresents  the thinking in the room and sways the conversation.

So unless you have a tapeworm, or a mouse in your pocket, or are pregnant, phrase your opinions as "I" messages: I think, I feel, I believe, I understand, I see it this way.

32.   It's okay to be afraid

> *Nothing in life is to be feared, it is only to be understood. Now is the time to understand more, so that we may fear less. (Marie Curie)*

Fear in the system will cause it to stop functioning for the reasons already mentioned. The leadership lesson here is that it is okay if there is fear in the system. Acknowledge it. Address it. Find out where it comes from.

Leaders should create a safe space so fear does not silence voices. Fear can't be dismissed. It comes from deep within each of us; it must be dealt with openly and honestly. Think back to when you were a child, afraid of monsters in the dark. It didn't matter how many times your parents turned on the light to show you that there were no monsters under the bed or in the closet; you  had to work your way through the fear; you had to come to know yourself that the monsters didn't exist. It is much the same process for adults.

Leaders can't make the fears go away. They can create the space in which the fears can be brought to light and a new level of understanding can be reached.

33.   Know who you are

He who knows others is wise. He who knows himself is enlightened. (Lao-Tzu)

Authenticity is part of this model of leadership. You have to show up each and every day as you and no one else.

To "know thyself" is to be honest with yourself about who you are, where you are, and what you want—without judgment or excuses. It is to be comfortable in your own skin; to be balanced in mind, body, and spirit; to embrace your uniqueness and individuality.

If the benefits to yourself are not enough, bear in mind that if others around you feel that you are not being yourself, they will not trust you. They will pick up on this because there will be an indication…

Remember those pesky mental models? What you are thinking will show in what you do—you will roll your

eyes, sigh, laugh, or send some "vibe" that lets others know
there is a disconnect between what you are thinking and
what you are saying. You are damned if you do, and
damned if you don't (those mental models will leak out),
so it's better to be honest about what you are thinking.

34. Know where you are and where you are going

"Would you tell me please, which way I ought to go from here?"

"That depends a good deal on where you want to get to," said the Cat. (Alice's Adventures in Wonderland)

To the person who does not know where he wants to go, there is no favorable wind. (Seneca)

Leadership is a journey. A journey has a beginning point and a destination. The beginning point is the here and now; the destination is the dream.

Take time to assess where you are in the here and now…

confirm the direction you need to take to reach the dream…

celebrate the distance you've come…

give thanks for the path yet to unfold.

35.   Rights vs. responsibilities

In dreams begin responsibility. (Yeats)

In western democratic culture, much ado is made about rights—what people are entitled to take—and little about responsibilities—what they should give.

H.G. Wells wrote an essay on human rights, and sent a request to Gandhi for an endorsement of the essay. Ghandi rejected the request by stating that he was not committed to human rights, but to human responsibility.

The reasoning he gave was that any group which demands its rights does so at the loss of the rights of some other group or part of society, the outcome would inevitably be that society would be torn apart as each person or group fought for their own rights. Ghandi commented that whatever rights we enjoy should be the result of the responsibilities we've committed to.

This rationale holds true for organizations, as subsystems of larger societal systems. There is much concern over the rights of employees and the obligations which leadership or the organization has to its employees. But seldom do leaders hold conversations with employees about the responsibilities employees can undertake to ensure rights for everyone in the organization.

Everyone in the organization, from the executive leaders down, shares responsibility in achieving the collective dream. Everyone has an individual responsibility to generate results from their individual assignments. Accountability, which can be used as a blame word, is best used when it means, "I have made a promise to myself or my team, and I will keep it."

Modifying one of our favorite quotes from the novel, Dune, we ask you to reflect on this litany against judgment as you work through the reflective questions:

I must not judge others.
Judgment is the mind killer.
Judgment is the little death that brings obliteration of other people.
I will face my judgment.
I will allow it to pass over me and through me as a powerful wave.
When it has gone, I will see it and its path.
Where judgment has gone, there will be nothing but learning.
Only I will remain to lead and learn.

Where do you find yourself wanting things for other people, professionally or personally?

How could you support those individuals to identify their personal visions of success?

How could you connect your vision of personal success to enable those individuals to achieve theirs?

In thinking about raising standards, identify the person you would claim is the poorest performer in the system under your purview. This person sets the proverbial standard for the team or division unless you are holding regular ongoing conversations about performance.

What kinds of conversations have you designed to bring this person's awareness to a new level?

Keeping in mind the need to integrate current reality and desired future, where are you influencing this person's creative tension?

What will you design moving forward to help this person develop creative tension?

Which practices do you employ during conversations and meetings that keep judgment of other people out of the learning field?

When you find yourself being defensive in a conversation or a meeting, how do you surface the fear that underlies that defensive posture? What have you done to respond effectively to judgment in conversations and meetings? What will you do going forward?

PART FIVE:
BEFORE WE SAY GOODBYE...

36.   The map is not the territory

Even with the best of maps and instruments, we can never fully chart our journeys. (Gail Pool)

Maps are made by people who have completed the journey, or at least enough of the journey to be able to create a guide for others.

When we pick up a map to use as a guide, even a good map, we will find that often the map does not accurately reflect the territory to be traveled. A road map, for instance, will give us a picture of the land to be traveled, possible routes, scenic stops and so forth. But it will not tell us about traffic jams or construction detours.

Some truths about the territory can only be learned by making the journey. So while the map is helpful, it cannot tell us all we need to know.

...it's only an inch...

This book is a kind of map. The principles contained within are based on our leadership journey—our reading, studying and practice.

But *our* journey is not *your* journey. And while our map, our model, may be a guide, what you encounter on your journey is yours alone to experience.

This is true of any model of living or leading you choose to adopt.

All models or representations are merely attempts to explain reality.

As such, all models are incomplete, because they are only representations of reality based on someone's mental models.

And, as such, all models are wrong.

They can help, guide, provide a means of measuring, but ultimately it is up to each person who adopts a model— this leadership model or any model—to take it and make it their own. Models are not one-size-fits-all; they must be tried, altered, and customized to each individual's needs, personalities, and preferences.

The danger in adopting any model in its entirety—and unquestioningly—is that models can become addictive, numbing us to possibilities. Models are attempts to frame what we know into a coherent order. At a deeper level, they are attempts to cope with innate existential confusion and with the overwhelming infinity of all that is possible.

37. We're making this up as we go

Imagination is more important than knowledge.
(Albert Einstein)

Because all **models are imperfect** (even this one), we continue our journey. Though we have a dream, we accept that it is *a* destination, not *the* destination.

This keeps us from becoming mired in certainty and thus keeps us open to the constant ebb and flow of systems, to shifting reality.

And we accept that **truth is a moving target**. Any idea, principle, or concept settled on today may be inaccurate or inadequate tomorrow once new information is known. So as leaders, we work under the assumption that things are true, here and now, but may not be tomorrow.

The path we are on today may change tomorrow.

The dream we hold today may change tomorrow.

The people who help us today may not be with us tomorrow, and people we do not even know will join us in our journey tomorrow.

38. Even the Lone Ranger had a partner

Never underestimate the power of a small group of committed people to change the world. In fact, it is the only thing that ever has. (Margaret Mead)

You can't do this work alone. It is essential that you find at least one partner, preferably two.

You will find that your journey is hard (but remember the only way out is through).

You will find allies along the way, but the journey will be easier if you bring your own, because…

> You will find that many people will resist the ideas; they are wrapped in the certainty they know best.

Many people will resist change…in you, in themselves, in the system.

> You will find yourself changing, as the practice of these leadership disciplines become part of you.

You may feel on the one hand challenged, unsettled, uncomfortable, discouraged…and on the other hand, grateful, enlightened, secure, even certain.

You may feel confusion as you delve deeply into the paradoxical nature of this work, this leadership practice that asks you to suspend certainty and be decisive,

> to be open to new ideas and to remain focused on a vision,

> to use a set of disciplines even though all models are wrong.

Having someone to share the experience with, someone who is undergoing the same feelings, will help you stay focused on your dream.

Having a partner gives you someone who speaks your language, who is leading the same way you are leading, who can share lessons from experience that may help you when you reach an impasse, and who can learn from you. Working with a partner creates a generative environment in which learning through conversation can occur. It gives you someone with whom you can model a leading and learning relationship.

The power of the relationship with your partner (or partners) that you create will be more powerful than you realize, and together you will be able to move mountains.

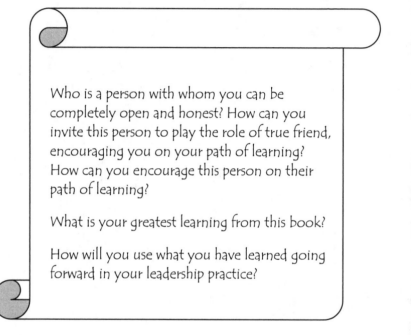

Who is a person with whom you can be completely open and honest? How can you invite this person to play the role of true friend, encouraging you on your path of learning? How can you encourage this person on their path of learning?

What is your greatest learning from this book?

How will you use what you have learned going forward in your leadership practice?

CLOSING THE
LEARNING LOOP...

I always knew that one day

I would take this road but

Yesterday

I did not know today

Would be the day.

(Nagarjuna)

Closing the learning loop is a way of ensuring that knowledge becomes wisdom, and as such is applied in daily practice. Closing the learning loop is our way of ensuring that you are able to use the thoughts in this book to create your own dream and a map to guide you in achieving your dream.

Learning is ultimately about changing behavior, gathering new knowledge to help you create and harvest...new relationships, new skills, new ideas. We have found in our experience that new behaviors become internalized when accompanied by a different way of thinking about and being in the world and by a new language to communicate the new experiences that arise.

Learning takes place through thinking, reflection, and action. Throughout this book, we have offered ideas for you to think about and to reflect upon. To crystallize the learning, it is now time that we offer you the opportunity put into action what you have learned.

The end of this book is the beginning of your personal leadership journey. To help you take the first step, we offer the following series of journal prompts modified from Otto Scharmer's *Theory U* automatic journaling exercise. We encourage you to use these questions as they were originally intended, as prompts for automatic writing.

Automatic writing allows you to bring to the surface deep responses before they are rationalized by the conscious mind. You should move through each question quickly, taking no more than a minute or two per question to write your thoughts. We have provided space for you to write your responses so this book can truly become a guide for you.

Think about various aspects of your life right now. What are the three or four most important challenges that your life (work and non-work) currently presents?

What are three or four accomplishments that you have achieved or competencies you have developed in your life?

What three or four aspirations, areas of interest, or undeveloped talents would you like to place more focus on in your future journey?

What are your most vital sources of energy?

How have the following three voices kept you from doing what you wanted to do: Voice of Judgment, Voice of Cynicsm, and Voice of Fear?

What it is that you want to create? What is your vision and intention for the next three to five years? Describe your dream as vividly and completely as possible.

What would you have to let go of in order to bring your vision into reality?

What in your current life provides the seeds for the future that you want to create?

Who in your current life can help you make your dream a reality?

What practical first steps will you take over the next three days to make your dream a reality?

What practical steps will you take over the next three months to make your dream a reality?

In order to determine the efficacy of any process, we build in a continuous improvement loop. What are some ways you have used this book that generated desired results? What are some ways you can use the book differently in the future?

Raymond D. Jorgensen, Ph.D.

has spent the past 30 years studying organizations and the concept of organizational change theories and parlayed this knowledge into the concept of Conversational Leadership, an insightful, theory-based method of conducting more effective meetings which taps into the collective wisdom of a group and leads to higher quality relationships for higher quality results. Ray consults, facilitates and conducts workshops for organizations on Conversational Leadership, with a proven track record of affecting organizational change. He has worked with public and private school systems, city and county governments, hospitals, banks, branches of the military, physicians' offices, and a variety of private businesses as a keynote speaker, facilitator, and seminar-workshop leader.

Ray spent thirty years in private and public schools as a teacher, coach, department head, collegiate faculty member, and school administrator.

He holds a Master of Science in Teaching and wrote a doctoral dissertation on learning organizations and organizational change. Best known to the school leaders in many states as the principal's principal, Ray has taught school administrators the practical knowledge necessary to both lead and manage which has brought measurable results and improvements within their school systems. During his three decades of public service, Ray was called upon by various communities to present seminars on both the technical and personal sides of leadership, management, and learning. These forays into public speaking defined Ray's work with various businesses and organizations and ultimately led to his current venture. Ray currently leads the team at JLC in conducting programs to affect organization change for both public and private organizations across the in a range of industries including technology, customer support, retail, healthcare, manufacturing, banking and financial services, insurance, telecommunications, state and local government, and education. Some of the organization's current clients include Chambers of Commerce, State Farm Insurance, Time Warner-AOL, IBM and other Fortune 1000 corporations.

Dena Hurst, Ph.D.

is a consultant for Jorgensen Learning Center and a practicing philosopher. In the course of her 15 years of consulting experience, she has studied theories and methods of leadership, governance, process improvement, performance management, and change. Using Conversational Leadership, Dena is able to bring a unique voice of guidance to those she serves and has a demonstrated ability to help individuals and organizations create and sustain change. Dena consults, lectures, and provides individualized coaching and guidance. Dena holds a bachelor's degree in Economics and a doctorate in Philosophy. Her research passion is leadership in the public sphere, and she has authored numerous book chapters, articles, and white papers. Her professional experience includes serving in the roles of project manager, project leader, research director, financial officer, and chief operations officer for a university outreach institute.

Her varied duties allowed her to work with government and university leaders at all levels, local and state elected officials, gubernatorial and legislative commissions, professional associations, and nonprofit organizations.

Dena also works to foster conversation among scholars around the globe. She recently coordinated a series of three international and interdisciplinary dialogue sessions in California, Australia and Czech Republic. She also volunteers for the Florida Association for Volunteer Action in the Caribbean and Americas (FAVACA) and has taught performance management and leadership skills to groups in Barbados, St. Kitts/Nevis, and Grenada. In May 2009, she was named FAVACA's Volunteer of the Year.

Jorgensen Learning Center

WHY JORGENSEN LEARNING CENTER (JLC)?

With JLC's Executive and Team Leadership Development Program comes a deeper understanding of enhanced leadership practices that will help your organization move toward the accomplishment of its shared dreams.

The JLC approach of Conversational Leadership blends learning and practice so that with each meeting, new knowledge on leadership principles and practices is introduced and learning conversations are designed to encourage participants to reflect together and find the shared meaning that connects to the desired results of the organization. Participants are also given the opportunity and support to practice what they are learning, both in each meeting and in the workplace.

JLC's Executive and Team Leadership Development Program unfolds along a recommended path, holding space for the individual needs of each organization.

"I learned about who I am and who I want to be as a leader. Most importantly, the experience engaged me in how to be a leader. The learning was deep and meaningful – even life altering. What an amazing experience! If you want to truly understand yourself and your role as a leader, how to break down organizational barriers, and how to unite a diverse group toward a common cause, then this is a program for you."

~CEO of a business consulting firm

FREQUENTLY ASKED QUESTIONS (FAQ'S)

Q: What does JLC do?

A: JLC provides project leadership and team development for schools and companies that, from time to time, need immediate access to proven leadership professionals who can step-in and enable leaders to effectively and efficiently lead critical projects or seamlessly add support on those already in-progress. Through this process, JLC develops internal executive, line and network leaders as excellent strategic practitioners and practical systems thinkers.

Q: What is JLC's leadership and team development? Why is it needed?

A: Simply stated, it's the ability to support leaders working on tough business and educational problems at any level by enabling them to successfully solve them in the fastest, most cost-effective way possible. Additionally, JLC develops leaders' internal capacity to identify and remove the structures causing and recreating the problems from the system. JLC assists leaders to efficiently and effectively work in and on the system.

Each week a project or program implementation lasts, it burns through more resources and distracts practitioners from their core work. At the same time, organizations suffer as some important desired outcomes have yet to be achieved. Typically, unsuccessful projects are attributable to weak leadership. JLC clients have found that paying for professional leadership development helps to shorten program initiation or project duration and achieve desired results more quickly.

Q: Why can't organizations just develop their own leaders?

A: Many organizations can develop their own leaders, however, even the largest and best-staffed sometimes lack opportunity and expertise necessary to develop true leaders who can effectively lead teams to accomplish assigned projects.

As leaders migrate through the system, they bring different styles to their work, and as such JLC supports the varying styles by focusing on the leadership disciplines necessary to accomplish organizational results.

In addition, JLC brings an outsider's perspective to a leadership development effort or project. Internal staff can often have trouble seeing across an organization or through murky internal politics. We see things with the filters turned off. We're also able to work outside the organizational chart to make sure internal leaders are enhancing their leadership capabilities and the right people are dealing with the right issues at the right times.

Q: What are some examples of typical JLC engagements?

A: JLC consults consist of executive and team leadership development as it relates to results oriented consulting, keynote presentations on the challenges of leadership and change, customized and individualized coaching, and personal leadership development seminars.

Conversational leadership, JLC's unique technology is the centerpiece of all of our JLC practices.

Examples of our consulting work might include aligning a team in a system that has lost focus, assisting an executive leader in understanding how they are seen by their direct reports, designing improvement plans for individuals and teams, assisting leaders in effectively responding to their teams, helping organizations 'keep the main thing the main thing' by identifying and removing distractions.

JLC keynotes use customized and highly interactive strategies to engage audiences in personalizing all the concepts delivered. Typically, clients identify useful 'take-aways' to bring back to their office, team or personal life.

Oftentimes organizations have a need to enhance a leaders current capacity to meet the challenges of organizational change. JLC assists these individuals by identifying how people see them in the current reality, their expectations for the future and provides customized ongoing support focusing on leadership capabilities needed to accomplish their desired results.

Our signature seminar series focuses on Tapping into the Spirit of Leading by highlighting core leadership capacities including personal development, leading in a living system, and leading teams.

"I asked the Jorgensen Learning Center to help me fortify a Leadership Team that I already believe in, so that they would have a 'safe space' to share, learn, discover, empathize, brainstorm, constructively criticize, and ultimately support each other even more. I also was looking for a way to re-infuse a culture of customer service, looking to examine how we operate at the most basic levels, and to seeing how our day-to-day thinking affects that dialogue and action with our customers. The facilitation and exercises were superb, compelling, and a rare commodity."

~ The Secretary of a Florida State Department.

Questions?
Comments?
Cries of Outrage?

Please contact us to share!

We would be honored if you would like
to order copies of this book to share with
your friends, colleagues, and
co-workers...just let us know!

Jorgensen Learning Center
Success is in the conversation.

www.GOJLC.com

info@GOJLC.com

2108 Park Avenue ◇ PMB #105 ◇ Orange Park, FL 32073

Phone: 904.264.9200 ◇ Fax: 904.297.3764